The Life of Jes

A Brief Insight

Written and Illustrated by
Emma J. Horsfield

This book is dedicated to all the wonderful and inspirational people I have met during my insightful journey of discovery into the life of Christ. This has resulted in my own new found faith in Christianity, which is now such an important part of my life. I will be always grateful for the experience and knowledge I have gained in this process, to which I have been led by my passion for art and the written word; gifts bestowed upon me by the Lord Himself.

Published by Peace Press Publishing

20 Chequerfield Avenue

Pontefract,

West Yorkshire

WF8 2TB

Printed and bound in GB

Introduction

A Brief Insight

'For God so loved the world that he gave his one and only Son, that whoever believes in him shall not perish but have eternal life' *(John 3:16).*

It may be difficult to believe but the sentiment within these words, written around two thousand years ago still evoke immense commitment and dedication from practising Christians around the globe. From a world population of seven billion, 2 billion are estimated to be Christian, a remarkable 28% of the world. But the rapid growth in Christianity in the developing world is coupled with the voracious rise in the modern world of atheism. Before embarking upon this exploratory journey into the life of Christ, I was a non-believer who knew very little about Christianity or religion in general. Being fed selected information by the media about how it contradicts modern science, along with the lack of Christian teaching in schools and general lack of spiritual acceptance within our society, have all certainly contributed to distorting my opinion on the subject of faith. I am now able to see that; to describe oneself as atheist is possibly a convenient escape mechanism. The label provides a means by which we can avoid confrontation with the issue of God, fulfilling the idea that it is easier to 'opt out' than to 'opt in'.

Adhering to standard practice in the 1970's, I was baptised as a young child and attended Sunday School, but never really considered myself a Christian, and knew very little about what Christianity entailed. Unfortunately this practice has declined rapidly in recent decades, meaning many people today never have the opportunity to become acquainted with the concept of attending Church. Despite my initial lack of connection with Christianity, I always felt humbled with an overwhelming sense of peace in places of worship, visiting Cathedrals and Churches regularly. However I now feel able to connect with them spiritually, as well as being attracted by the historicity and visual splendour, which is a huge bonus.

To believe in and accept God into our lives requires effort, dedication and spiritual commitment - resulting in a complete change of lifestyle. To believe in something is invariably to have understanding of it on some level, and to have that understanding requires elementary interest and curiosity. Initially inspired by my passion for art and painting, the subject of Christianity and Jesus was something I stumbled upon quite by accident. Research into inspirational historical artists, such as Caravaggio and Botticelli, led me to realise that artists painted subject matter largely based on Biblical themes. This ignited a spark of interest within me as I wondered how I would interpret these themes in my own artistic practice. Of course, knowing very little about the Bible meant I had to engage in a great deal of research; enabling me to develop an understanding of the historic story of Jesus, and what his life signified. I unashamedly purchased a children's Bible, (The Lion Bible for Children: *see Further Reading section*) which enabled me to quickly become acquainted with the Bible stories. I read this every day and found myself becoming more and more interested to learn about Christianity in more depth.

Once I finished reading this book of Bible stories I embarked upon a torrent of discovery via internet Bible study sites, while also purchasing more books as my curiosity grew, including three full Bible versions. Simultaneously I began painting 'The Life of Jesus Christ' exhibition; after completing around five of these paintings, I also became inspired to write this short book about his life and teachings. I tried to keep in mind a quote I had read, "A Christian should use these arts to the glory of God... not just as tracts...but as things of beauty to the praise of God" *(Schaeffer, 2006)*. Schaeffer's writings suggest that not only should art be used for the glorification of God but that it should also be something of beauty, as beauty is also pleasing to God. He goes on to explain about the many examples of God instructing Moses in Exodus, as to how the Temple, tabernacle and even priest's garments should be decorated. The Bible demonstrates that the purpose of art in these areas is for beauty. Messages in the Bible are often misinterpreted, as can be seen in passages in *Leviticus 26:1, Exodus 20:4 and Deuteronomy 4:6*. Here, when God commands that no idols or images should be made, it can be understood as referring to the worship of idols, rather than adoration from an aesthetic perspective. Art; whether painting, prose, music or dance is intrinsically linked to Christianity, and all the arts can be used for the glorification of God. If God created the earth and everything within it, including the human as a whole, it therefore stands to reason that he has also bestowed upon us talents and intellect, that we may use them for his pleasure.

At 39, the light of Jesus entered my life.

'The true light that gives light to everyone was coming into the world. He was in the world, and though the world was made through him, the world did not recognise him. He came to that which was his own, but his own did not receive him. Yet to all who did receive him, to those who believed in his name, he gave the right to become children of God' *(John 1: 9-12).*

It happened at a time when I was open to him both intellectually and spiritually, and I can now see this is the best possible way to find God: a personal desire and interest resulting in authentic faith and acceptance. It is worth bearing in mind that the journey of life and its trials and tribulations mean that we can all find God when we feel ready and it is never too late. Ideologies relevant to Christianity I have always held dear, pertain to Jesus' teachings: we have no right to judge others and every human life is equal. We all have our own unique journey in life, with many prospective directions and so must make our own choices.

Since its very beginning, Christianity has had to deal with scepticism and widespread opposition. Feeling a lack of strength recently, I opened my Bible at *Isaiah 45,* and saw the first words on the page: ***"I have equipped you for battle."*** As I read further I also found: ***'[The people will declare], "the Lord is the source of all my righteousness and strength"'*** *(Isaiah*

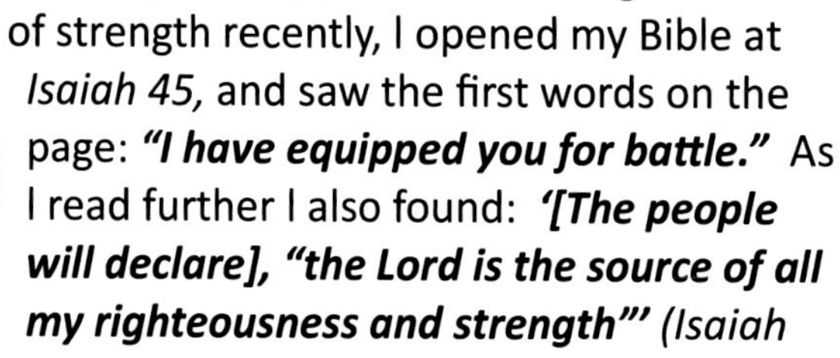

45:24). I took great deal of encouragement from this and realised the Lord was working with me to complete my endeavours with his exhibitions and books. I began to realise that God has always been there for me, equipping me with the strength to cope in difficult times.

Although faith is a recent discovery for me, I hope I have done Jesus justice and that others gain some enjoyment from viewing my art and reading my books. I have learned countless lessons while aboard this academic, spiritual journey of discovery and artistic creation, and envisage a lifetime of learning ahead. When entering into a relationship with God, we need to open our minds and hearts fully, not be tainted by pre-conceptions. Since discovering Jesus, my learning is a constant process which I thoroughly enjoy, and I would certainly encourage others to join me in my quest for wisdom. ***"Blessed are those who hunger and thirst for righteousness, for they will be filled"*** *(Matthew 5:6).*

God has endowed us with moral values so that we use this ability to strive for ethical justice, always seeking to do what we know deep down to be right.

I hope you enjoy reading this book and please note, I post all updates onto my blog which can be linked to via my website:

www.emmahorsfield.com

(All quotes in this book are taken from the New International Version Bible, so I use lower case pronouns throughout when referring to the

Lord (e.g. him, he). Although traditionally Christ's pronouns would be in upper case, the contemporary approach is to use lower case for the sake of grammatical correctness and flow. I also describe the narrative in present tense, reflective of the omnipresence of our Lord, while the direct quotes may remain in the past tense as they are written in the Bible).

Blessings everyone.

A Brief Insight.

"I am the way and the truth and the life. No one comes to the Father except through me" *(John 14:6).*

When I read this statement from Jesus, my desire to understand its meaning propelled me into a crusade of spiritual discovery and learning about his life. This is a person so important that he divided history into two: the period before his birth and the period after it, and even two thousand years after his death his followers keep on growing.

Although it would be logical to assume that Jesus was born in the year 0 AD, it is commonly accepted among historians that in fact it was more likely to be 6 – 4 BC. In the Gospel according to Luke, the angel Gabriel appears to teenager Mary who is engaged to carpenter Joseph. Scholars have determined Mary to be between the ages of thirteen and 16; an age which may seem remarkably immature to us in the modern world, but in ancient times would be normal for girls to experience marriage and childbirth.

The angel explains that Mary is to be visited by the

Holy Spirit:
"Do not be afraid Mary, for you have found favour with God. You will conceive and give birth to a son, and you are to call him Jesus" *(Luke: 1: 30-31).*
"He will be great, and will be called the Son of the Most High. The Lord God will give him the throne of his father David; He will reign over Jacob's descendants forever—his kingdom will never end" *(Luke 1: 32-33).*

Gabriel explains Jesus' divine status as the 'Son of God' and later, Mary is reluctant about sharing the news. Joseph has reservations about the situation; after all Mary is expecting a child not conceived through him, and there is a great stigma attached to unmarried mothers. However, Joseph is informed in a dream that what Mary says is true: She will indeed be the mother of the Saviour. Understandably astonished and confused having never experienced intimacy, Mary wonders why she has been chosen but feels humbled to have been so.

Luke's Gospel explains that Joseph and Mary make the journey from Nazareth to Bethlehem under the orders of Roman rule, where they will register for the Census of Quirinius. This is Joseph's birthplace so he feels confident he will find them a place to stay for the night, especially considering Mary is heavily pregnant. However, their lengthy search is in vain:

'While they were there [in Bethlehem], the time came for the baby to be born, and she gave birth to her first-born, a son. She wrapped him in cloths and placed him in a manger – because there was no guest

The Annunciation

room available for them' *(Luke 2:6).*
'For to us a child is born, to us a son is given, and the government will be on his shoulders. And he will be called Wonderful Counsellor, Mighty God, Everlasting Father, Prince of Peace' *(Isaiah 9:6).*

Jesus is born in a stable cave, the only shelter his parents can find: it is here where he begins his life on earth in the most humblest of beginnings. Purity and 'heaven on earth' born within the deprivation and squalor of a cold, windswept cave. Later, King Herod and the persecutors don't think to search for him there, as they would not expect to find divinity in such a place. They likely feel that if he is the Son of God, then he must be born into opulence and comfort; after all would the Lord not want this for his own son?

From a theological perspective we can see that with this birth, Mary is vindicating the sin and temptation of Eve in Genesis, by bringing into the world he who will die for sinners. Eve was tempted and disobeyed, giving birth to sin; Mary believes and obeys, giving birth to salvation in the form of Christ. It is widely accepted that the Messiah is coming and this is referred to in the scriptures many times.

Mary knows early on that her son will suffer greatly, be taken from her, and in turn she will also experience immense pain, but her humility and willing participation in this ensures her own saintly place in the Holy family. Not being married to Mary when

The Nativity: The Holy Family

she becomes pregnant with a child who is not his, Joseph humbly accepts responsibility for this woman and child many others would deny. He cares for Mary and the child thereafter, looking upon Jesus as his own son. His selfless participation shows Joseph's faith and trust in God and his true love for Mary, thus ensuring his own special position in the Holy family.

After Jesus is born, an angel appears in the dark night while shepherds are watching their sheep. The angel informs them of the birth of the Saviour and that he lay in an animal feeding trough (known as a 'manger' in biblical texts). The shepherds are alarmed but are told they have nothing to fear as their Saviour is born.

'Suddenly a great company of the heavenly host appeared with the angel, praising God and saying, "Glory to God in the highest heaven, and on earth peace to those on whom his favour rests."
When the angels had left them and gone into heaven, the shepherds said to one another, "Let's go to Bethlehem and see this thing that has happened, which the Lord has told us about"' *(Luke 2: 13-15).*

The shepherds find Jesus in the place the angels tell them about, and they praise God for what he has brought to earth.

Sometime after his birth, which scholars claim could be up to two years later, the 'Magi' come to visit Jesus. They travel many miles to Jerusalem from the east bearing symbolic gifts for him. With these offerings they are able to prove their faith and respect for the

The Nativity: The Shepherds Arrive

child they already know to be the Son of God. Although the Bible doesn't actually state there are *three* wise men, the plural 'Magi' indicates there are at least two, and their bringing three gifts indicates three individuals. It is quite remarkable that these obviously powerful and wealthy men travel such a great journey so that they may bow down to a baby. Their clear faith is unwavering and unequivocal.

'On coming to the house, they saw the child with his mother Mary, and they bowed down and worshipped him. Then they opened their treasures and presented him with gifts of gold [representing Kingship] frankincense [as a sign of his priesthood] and myrrh [to signify his predicted death and embalming]' *(Matthew 2:11).*

When Roman King Herod learns of the birth of Jesus and the coming of the Magi, he becomes alarmed and, feeling his power threatened decides to find the child. Deceptively he tells the Magi:

"Go and search carefully for the child. As soon as you find him, report to me, so that I too may go and worship him" *(Matthew 2:7).*

Herod is deceiving them but God informs the wise men in a dream that they should not return to Herod. However in the meantime Herod is so intent on discovering Jesus' whereabouts and disposing of him that he

The Nativity: The Magi visit

orders the murder of all baby boys under the age of two years old. Compliant with the information previously given to him by the Magi, he is sure this will eradicate any chance of Jesus' survival. Herod, deeply disliked and resented by the Jews, partly because of his ancestry, is generally known as being a cruel ruler, an identity which he clearly proves with his murderous act: 'The Massacre of the Innocents'. The world Jesus is born into is filled with sin. It is a place where it is acceptable for unwanted babies to be left out on the street to die, political corruption thrives and gladiators are murdered to provide public entertainment. Jesus wants to teach people to care for each other and treat others as they would be treated in return: a difficult task when the culture of violence, slavery and persecution is so widespread and tolerated.

Significantly, four hundred years earlier, prophet Malachi reveals in the Old Testament that before Jesus is born there will be another to prepare the way for Jesus' entry to the world. We now know this is 'John the Baptist', Jesus' cousin, who is born six months before him *(Luke 1:36).*

Herod fails to locate Jesus and an angel of the Lord comes to Joseph in a dream, instructing him to take Mary and the baby to Egypt where they will be safe. Joseph obeys and the Holy family remain there until Herod is confirmed deceased, after which the rule of Palestine under Roman authority is divided between

Madonna and Child:
Ultimate symbol of peace

his three sons.
Jesus' arrival on earth is expected and has been predicted many times, including in the Old Testament over seven hundred years earlier:

"But you, Bethlehem Ephrathah,
though you are small among the clans of Judah, out of you will come for me one who will be ruler over Israel, whose origins are from of old, from ancient times"
(Micah 5:2).

Jesus' coming is even referred to as the 'Universal Wise Man yet to come' *(Sheen, 2008)* by Socrates and Plato. The people of the world are expecting the Messiah and it is the numerous prophecies which can distinguish Christ from founders of all other world religions. No other person's birth has been foreseen before or since: It is an incarnation of universal expectation. Even King Herod knows Jesus the Son of God Almighty has arrived, or in pursuit of protecting his own power and glory, would not be so determined to kill him. Human beings are born to live, whereas Jesus is born to die, a fact separating him further from mere mortals. The purpose of his life is Saviour of humanity.

Simeon, described as a devout, righteous man with the presence of the Holy Spirit, tells Mary that her son will divide men; that they will either love him or hate him depending upon their inner soul, and the reflection they see of themselves when they look at him. Simeon is told by the Holy Spirit that he will not see death before he has seen Jesus the Saviour. He is directed to the Temple that day by the Holy Spirit so that he may see him, and finds peace in preparation for the end of his earthly life.

'Then Simeon blessed them and said to Mary, his mother: "This child is destined to cause the falling and rising of many in Israel, and to be a sign that will be spoken against, so that the thoughts of many hearts will be revealed. And a sword will pierce your own soul too"' *(Luke 2: 34-35).*

This must be a terrifying thought for Mary, and every mother's worst nightmare. How could she contemplate the suffering which was to come?

The circumcision of eight day old Jesus is his first major bloodshed in his lifetime. The tradition of this procedure goes back to *Genesis 17:* the practice being part of the covenant between God and Abraham. There will follow six other significant examples of Jesus' bloodshed over the duration of his earthly existence: Agony in the Garden, Scourging, Crowning of Thorns, The Way of the Cross, Crucifixion and the Piercing of his Heart *(Sheen, 2012).* Since the times of the Old Testament bloodshed is the signifier of sacrifice and cleansing.

After his circumcision, there is no mention of Jesus again until he is twelve years old, during which time we are told that he grows; this growth meaning not just physically but also spiritually and emotionally, in preparation for the events to come.

The Gospel of Luke *(2)* explains that Jesus and his parents visit the Temple in Jerusalem, as they always do for the Feast of the Passover: commemoration for the liberation of the Israelites, led from Egypt by Moses in the Old Testament. Once the days of the feast end, Mary and Joseph travel home, believing that Jesus is with them, but when they realise he isn't there they return to Jerusalem to try and find him. Three days later they find him in the Temple conversing with teachers, who are amazed at how knowledgeable the young boy is and at the things he says. Mary asks her son why he would cause them worry like this, to which Jesus replies,

'"Why were you searching for me? Didn't you know that I had to be in my Father's house?" But they did not understand what he was saying to them' *(Luke 2: 50).*

Jesus is clearly displaying his wisdom and developing maturity, demonstrating to Mary that the Lord is his father so he is in his house at the Temple. Although Mary and Joseph are his earth parents, the Lord God holds the highest position in his life.

When instructed by his parents to come with them he obediently follows back home to Nazareth, but the traumatic experience has a great effect on Mary. She must feel great fear and terror at the suffering she knows is yet to come. Notably, despite his power and glory Jesus displays constant obedience in all he does on the earth; obedience to God and God's will, to his parents and in his submission and acceptance of his fate.

After twelve years of age, many years pass by with no further word about Jesus. We are told again simply; that Jesus grows wiser and stronger and becomes more and more in favour with God.

'And the Child grew and became strong in spirit, filled with wisdom; and the grace of God was upon Him' *(Luke 2:40).*

The eighteen years that pass from the age from twelve to thirty remain subject to widespread speculation, as his life is unexplained. Various claims have been made to suggest that Jesus travels to India and even Britain, learning from other religions around the world. However, as we have gleaned from the last reference to his age, at just twelve years old, the leaders are already marvelling at his knowledge. The reference in *Matthew (13:55),*

"Isn't this the carpenter's son? Isn't his mother's name Mary, and aren't his brothers James, Joseph, Simon and Judas?"

could lead the reader to assume that since the last point of reference to his age, he simply works as a carpenter in his home town of Nazareth; as for generations it is normal practice for boys to follow in the profession of their fathers. Being a carpenter, it is perhaps ironic that he spends his life at work with tools and wood which will later be used to torture and crucify him.

We may wonder why there is no information in the Bible about Jesus from the age of twelve until he reveals himself as the Messiah. However, in the time these records were made this would be normal practice. In ancient times people were only judged by their character based on the last few years of their lives. This could explain why much of the New Testament is given to detailing the last three years of Jesus' life, as this is the time scale of his public ministry. There may not be anything of relevance to record about the missing eighteen years, so the focus is on describing the most important and relevant events. The significance of these unknown years play an important role in Judaism however; twelve / thirteen being traditionally adopted as the age of a child's Bar Mitzvah and 30 the age of acceptance into priesthood. It should also be noted that after the eighteen year long Biblical gap, there is no further mention of Joseph. After this Jesus is also known as being the 'Son of Mary', suggesting his father must be deceased, or Jesus would still be referred to as 'Son of Joseph'.

When he is thirty years old, in Galilee on the River Jordan, Jesus follows God's will and asks John the Baptist to baptise him:

'Then Jesus came from Galilee to the Jordan to be baptised by John. But John tried to deter him, saying, "I need to be baptised by you, and do you come to me?" Jesus replied, "Let it be so now; it is proper for us to do this to fulfil all righteousness." So John consented. As soon as Jesus was baptised, he went up out of the water. At that moment heaven was opened, and he saw the Spirit of God descending like a dove and alighting on him. And a voice from heaven said, "This is my Son, whom I love; with him I am well pleased"' *(Matthew 3:*

The Baptism of Christ

13-17). In his baptism, Christ shares in the sins and guilt of humanity and is at one with them. He chooses to do this for he does not need to be cleansed or to repent, but in doing so becomes a full member of the human race. Being without sin means he also remains divine. After he is baptised, the Holy Spirit in the form of a dove appears, (the only time in the Bible this occurs): the dove consequently becomes a symbol of peace and harmony, and remains so to this day. The Baptism event signals the end of Christ's privacy, as he has kept his mission away from the public eye until this moment. Now he is there for all to witness and his public ministry begins.

After his baptism on the River Jordan, Jesus is led by the Holy Spirit into the wilderness and here he starves for forty days and forty nights. He chooses to suffer and be at one with the human race he loves so much, learning what it is like to be hungry, as the poor starving people on earth do. He is at one with their suffering and is able to empathise and have genuine understanding. The devil tries to tempt Jesus into using his power to save himself but Jesus says defiantly,

"It is written: Man shall not live on bread alone, but on every word that comes from the mouth of God" *(Matthew 4:4).*

So the devil takes Jesus to the Temple in Jerusalem and tells him to jump from the great height, as it is written in the scriptures, that angels will save him if he falls,

'He has put his angels in charge of you. They will catch you in their hands so that you will

not hit your foot on a rock" *(Psalm 91:11–12).*

Jesus wisely replies that it also states in the scriptures that we should not test the Lord. After this the devil leads Jesus to a high mountain and tells him that if he worships *him*, he will be rewarded with all the lands and kingdoms. Jesus refuses, saying that in the scriptures it is clear that one God only shall be worshipped, and that is the Lord. Unlike Adam in Eden, Jesus never succumbs to temptation, always remaining pure and divine, untainted by the sin of humanity. He knows this is the path he must follow and such sufferings as the forty day fast are preparation for the even greater pain he endures later. His amazing power does not allow him to use these gifts for his own benefit, even though he later uses them to heal others, perform miracles of wine and bread and for raising a child from the dead. We can begin to see how, in his humility and selflessness this divine human connects heaven and earth with his very existence.

After hearing that John the Baptist is imprisoned, Jesus returns to Galilee where he begins to preach and select those he wants for his followers. By Lake Galilee he finds Simon (later to be known as Peter) and his brother Andrew, and two other brothers James and John. From there he goes all over Galilee preaching the good news of the kingdom of heaven and healing the sick. News of Jesus spreads all over Syria and people bring those to be healed by him with all kinds of illnesses. In 'The Sermon on the Mount', he tells his followers:

"Blessed are you when people insult you,

persecute you and falsely say all kinds of evil against you because of me. Rejoice and be glad, because great is your reward in heaven, for in the same way they persecuted the prophets who were before you" *(Matthew 5:11-12).*

Jesus tells us that we should not allow non-believers to destroy our faith with insults and mockery, as our endurance will be rewarded. He continues to teach the people about the importance of law, and of the sins of anger, sexual sin and adultery, of giving, worshipping, prayer and money. He tells them that they should not judge others, and they should treat them how they too wish to be treated.

Now known as *The Lord's Prayer*, Jesus explains how people should pray:

"This, then, is how you should pray:
Our Father in heaven, hallowed be your name, your kingdom come, your will be done, on earth as it is in heaven. Give us today our daily bread. And forgive us our debts, as we also have forgiven our debtors. And lead us not into temptation, but deliver us from the evil one. For if you forgive other people when they sin against you, your heavenly Father will also forgive you. But if you do not forgive others their sins, your Father will not forgive your sins" *(Matthew 6: 9-15).*

In all his work on earth Jesus seeks to teach people about humility and honesty both with themselves and with others. The Lord knows they who are genuine and we should not seek to receive sympathy from others or publicise our sacrifices. Those of us who give quietly and without physical reward or recognition are those who God knows to be true. Jesus offers an example by telling his followers that when fasting they should not display their discomfort to others as this will not bring them their reward. Jesus is equally silent about his own power until the beginning of his ministry, and asks those he heals not to inform others about what he has done.

In Cana in Galilee, Jesus and Mary are in attendance at a wedding party, when Mary informs him they have run out of wine; a seemingly insignificant problem in today's world but during that time would have been very shameful and offensive to the guests. It is even suggested by some scholars that this could be a reason for litigation; clearly indicating it is not something to be taken lightly. In notifying Jesus of this situation it is clear that Mary wants her son to do something, although she refrains from specifying what she expects him to do. It is here that Jesus performs his first miracle of turning water into wine, an act which gains him many more followers and believers in his glory *(John 2: 1-11)*.

Jewish leaders do not openly accept Jesus being the Son of God and, like King Herod feel threatened by his presence. After listening to his teachings, one night a leader of the Jews, Pharisee Nicodemus visits Jesus in Jerusalem. He knows others will condemn him for it but Nicodemus feels the truth exists in Jesus and wants to know more from him. He believes in him, and knowing the risks of public exposure, visits at night in the quest for enlightenment. Jesus tells him:

"For God did not send his Son into the world to condemn the world, but to save the world through him. Whoever believes in him is not condemned, but whoever does not believe stands condemned already because they have not believed in the name of God's one and only Son" *(John 3:17-18).*

When visiting the country of Samaria Jesus speaks with a woman near a well. Something which sets Jesus apart from the ordinary man is his insight, and the way he knows things which can't be known. He knows the woman has had five husbands and when she tells him she now has no husband, Jesus knows her to be truthful. The woman, who realises this is the expected Messiah, spreads the news about him, encouraging others in turn to follow Jesus. Many of the Samaritans in that town believe in Jesus because of what the woman says:

"He told me everything I ever did" *(John 4: 39).*

Later, when healing a man at Bethesda, Jerusalem, the Jews seek all the more to kill him. They believe he not only breaks the Sabbath, but is also claiming to be the Son of God, making himself equal with God *(John 5: 18).* This claim would amount to blasphemy which, at this time carries a penalty of stoning to death. People seem always afraid of what they don't understand and quickly judge those they have no right to judge. Jesus teaches against this behaviour and these perfect moral attributes all contribute to his success in being the one and only Son of God in a human body.

The miracle of Jesus feeding the five thousand is the only miracle present in all four gospels except the ascension, meaning the authors all thought this was a major significant event in the Christian story. The disciples, even though they have borne witness to Jesus performing miracles many times before, cannot believe that five loaves and two fish will feed so many people. Of course Jesus has the power to feed all these people himself, but he delegates the task to his disciples. He knows they must feel trust in God for this to work and without true faith they will not be provided with the food. His test proves fruitful and all the people, who some Bible scholars suggest could be more like 20,000 people, are fed and there is even some left over. This demonstrates that God can provide far more than we imagine when there is faith,

'Now to him who is able to do immeasurably more than all we ask or imagine, according to his power that is at work within us' *(Ephesians 3:20).*

Jesus practices what he preaches: despite his divine high status he does not discriminate against commonly less valued members in society, like human beings do. He enlists fishermen with little knowledge as his disciples; people who would ordinarily command little respect in the community. He treats all people with the same amount of respect and grace. His treatment of women at the time is controversial, as women are seen as second class to their male counterparts. However Jesus treats them as equals. He gracefully allows a 'sinful' woman to wash his feet, knowing she has genuine faith and goodness within her, saying to the woman,

"Your faith has saved you. Go in peace" *(Luke 7: 50).*

A most interesting example of Jesus' wisdom and compassion is seen when he visits the Mount of Olives. He is asked by a group of men what should be done to a woman caught in the act of adultery, for which the punishment is stoning to death. When they continue asking him, he lifts himself up, and says to them,

"Let any one of you who is without sin be the first to throw a stone at her" *(John 8: 7).*

Needless to say the men walk away in shame and the woman is saved. Jesus demonstrates his forgiveness and tells her to go and sin no more, as although aware of humans' sinful nature he also knows they can repent and change for the better.

'Jesus commands us to love one another as he loves us' *(John 13:34).*

Jesus is never afraid for himself, always trusting God to know what is right and has total faith in his will. When Jesus is on earth, leprosy is a much feared disease and those inflicted with it are avoided and ostracised from mainstream society. People scorn those with leprosy due to fearing for their own safety. However, when Jesus is 31 years old a man with the disease comes to him asking for healing, if he is willing. Jesus reaches out his hand and touches the man saying,

'"I am willing. Be clean," and immediately the man is healed from his disease' *(Matthew 8: 3).*

In the Gospel according to Matthew *(10)*, Jesus gives authority to heal, to all his twelve apostles, which by now also include Bartholomew, Philip, Matthew, Thomas, Thaddeus, James the Less, Judas Iscariot and Simon the Zealot. We know very little about the disciples, only that some of them have a background in fishing and Matthew in tax collecting: the emphasis of the Gospels being placed on the most important figure of Jesus and his ministry. Details not pertaining to his teachings are treated as less relevant.

Jesus leads a very simplistic life in terms of his outlook and the activities he takes part in. He does not see the rich or wealthy as being believers and followers of him, arguing that they could use their wealth to help the poor if they are true, rather than squander it on themselves. One event in the Bible where we can see an example of this is when he expels money lenders from the Temple, telling the crowd,

"It is written, 'My house shall be called a house of prayer,' but you make it a den of robbers" *(Matthew 21:13).*

He sees them as benefiting from others' misfortune and disrespecting the house of the Lord. Such activities do not have their place in the sacred place of worship, which is kept for the glory of God.

There is a Jewish leader of the synagogue called

Jairus, who, unlike the other leaders, puts his trust in Jesus, coming begging for help as his daughter is dying. Jesus comes and everyone is crying as they believe she is dead, but Jesus revives her, and the twelve year old girl stands up and walks. Jesus, retaining his humility, instructs them not to tell anyone else about this *(Mark 5: 37-43).* Had Jairus not truly believed in Jesus being the Son of God, his daughter would surely not have lived. Lies and insincerity are apparent to God, thus without faith, healing cannot take place.

Jesus tells his followers of his own inevitable death and that they should sacrifice their body to save their soul,

"Truly I tell you, some who are standing here will not taste death before they see the kingdom of God" *(Luke 9:27).*

He indicates they will not need to die before witnessing him rising to heaven. Here he demonstrates that the earthly life is not the only one we have and once we reach death our souls will still endure.

'About eight days after Jesus says this, he takes Peter, John and James with him and goes up onto a mountain to pray. As he is praying, the appearance of his face changes and his clothes become as bright as a flash of lightning. Two men, Moses and Elijah, appear in glorious splendour, talking with Jesus. They speak about his departure, which he is about to bring to fulfilment at Jerusalem' *(Luke 9: 28-31).*

'The Transfiguration' depicts the moment where Christ becomes light and his body

The Transfiguration - Jesus, Moses and Elijah

shines, on the mountain with John, James and Peter. Elijah and Moses appear and are equally dazzling white. This event is the turning point from which Christ makes his way to Jerusalem to suffer humiliation and death, but it is because of the glory he experiences at the transfiguration that he is able to face the pain and suffering of the cross.

Jesus' 'Agony in the Garden', hours before he is due to be executed, is so extreme that he is told to have sweated blood; physically symbolising his emotional torture and sacrifice. Being the Messiah, he knows in intimate detail everything that will befall him. He knows he will be tortured, beaten and crucified and this knowledge of impending physical pain is further enhanced by the emotional pain of knowing one of his beloved disciples will betray him, and that those who earlier had called him their Messiah, will shout for his crucifixion. He pains at the lack of human faithfulness and how their selfish whims can so easily be used to betray the Lord.

'The Last Supper' is a biblical reminder of the sacrifice of the Passover where Jesus predicts Judas Iscariot's betrayal and Peter's denial of him. It is where Jesus and his twelve disciples eat their last meal together and he tells them of the bodily sacrifice he will make for the sins of humanity. Jesus gives Judas the opportunity to save himself but Judas chooses to leave the meal early and does not change his mind about what he is to do. Jesus' main concern at the Supper is not for himself but

for those who follow him and their safety, with the knowledge that his work on earth is almost finished. He will soon face the physical and emotional suffering he came into the world to endure.

Many paintings depict this scene and it is particularly illustrated in Italian Renaissance art; artistic license meaning many variations on the scene have been created. All we know from the Gospels is that Jesus and his twelve apostles are seated at the table. We do not know if anyone else is there or not, or if anyone else is present but not seated at the table. Some believe Mary Magdalene is present, who is often depicted at his feet. As tradition requires for a meal to be preceded by feet washing, this is certainly possible, especially as she was possibly his dearest follower.

'When evening came, Jesus was reclining at the table with the Twelve. And while they were eating, He said, "Truly I tell you, one of you will betray me." They were very sad and began to say to Him one after the other, "Surely you don't mean me, Lord?" Jesus replied, "The one who has dipped his hand into the bowl with me will betray me. The Son of Man will go just as it is written about him. But woe to that man who betrays the Son of Man! It would be better for him if he had not been born"' *(Matthew 26: 20-24).*

His prediction comes true as Judas proceeds to return the thirty pieces of silver he received for identifying Jesus and, unable to cope with his deplorable act, commits suicide. Once captured after Judas' betrayal, Jesus is mercilessly beaten and scourged, a savage method of torture involving multiple lashes with whips and canes which are festooned with attachments such as metal and other sharp objects. Pilate, the Roman ruler, offers the people the opportunity to allow Jesus to be released after his scourging but they still call for his crucifixion, and even choose for profound murderer Barabbas, to be released in his place. Jesus' fate is sealed and the hour which he came into the world to suffer is upon him.

Crucifixion is known to have been the most painful method of execution given to the most hated and evil people; being so painful that the word 'ex***cruci***ating' derives directly from it. Jesus is forced to carry his cross to the place outside the city walls known as Golgotha (Skull) after his relentless beating and torture by the Roman soldiers. He must be suffering extreme physical agony but refuses the myrrh concoction offered to him to dull the pain before the crucifixion. He wants to be in charge of his senses and feel full suffering for the sins of man.

'Above his head they placed the written charge against him: "This is Jesus, the King of the Jews". "He saved others,' they said, "but he can't save himself! He's the king of

The Crucifixion

Israel! Let him come down now from the cross, and we will believe in him"' *(Matthew 27: 37, 42).*

In the final minutes of his life Jesus in his desperation and agony is noted as repeating the Psalm of David which predicts his coming a thousand years earlier. He cries a heart wrenching plea,

"Eli, Eli, lema sabachthani?", which translates as, ***"My God, My God, why have you forsaken me?"****(Matthew 27:46).*

It is here where Jesus experiences his truly darkest hour, the feeling of abandonment and desolation from God. He is taking the ultimate punishment for the sins of man and for they who rejected the Lord, and is now suffering the same rejection. He is feeling abandoned by both heaven and earth.

'Near the cross of Jesus stood his mother, his mother's sister, Mary the wife of Clopas, and Mary Magdalene. When Jesus saw his mother there, and the disciple whom he loved standing nearby, he said to her, "Woman, here is your son," and to the disciple, "Here is your mother." From that time on, this disciple took her into his home' *(John 19: 25-27).*

Jesus offers his closest disciple to his mother so that he may care for her and that she can still feel a mother – son relationship. In his final darkest moments he is still thinking of the people he loves. He even forgives one of the criminals crucified alongside him, saying that he will see him in heaven.

The Crucifixion: Mary Magdalene and Mother Mary in embrace

Although there is no mention of what is known as *'The Pieta'* in the Gospels, where Mary is alone with her son after his descent from the cross, it is a great source of inspiration to artists and has been depicted many times over the centuries. More often an iconic image of the Catholic faith in which the Mother Mary is highly venerated and a focus of prayer, the image provokes pity for the mother of a son and displays how together they share their suffering, which they endure for him to be Saviour.

'The Lord is close to the broken hearted and saves those who are crushed in spirit' *(Psalm 34:18).*

'He will wipe every tear from their eyes. There will be no more death or mourning or crying or pain, for the old order of things has passed away' *(Revelation 21: 4).*

Jesus is recorded as having died on the Friday, but on Monday morning when Mary Magdalene and the women go to visit Jesus' tomb with spices *(Matthew 28:1)*, they are shocked of course to find it empty.

'On the first day of the week, very early in the morning, the women took the spices they had prepared and went to the tomb. They found the stone rolled away from the tomb, but when they entered, they did not find the body of the Lord Jesus. While they were wondering about this, suddenly two men in

The Pieta: Mother and Son

clothes that gleamed like lightning stood beside them. In their fright the women bowed down with their faces to the ground, but the men said to them, "Why do you look for the living among the dead? He is not here; he has risen! Remember how he told you, while he was still with you in Galilee: 'The Son of Man must be delivered over to the hands of sinners, be crucified and on the third day be raised again." Then they remembered his words' *(Luke 24: 1-8).*

The resurrection is the crucial event sceptics have difficulty believing about the life of Christ; the moment where Jesus proves his victory over sin, persecution and death. It is something incomprehensible to humans and which could only occur in the presence of divinity. There are though a number of factors which can explain that this event occurred *(see Epilogue).*

Jesus had told the disciples of his impending suffering: that he would be crucified, and that he would rise on the third day. Although they knew not what he meant at the time, they took note of his words *(Matthew 16:21).* But despite this prediction by he who they believe to be the Son of God, the apostles, displaying human volatility as opposed to the divine stability of Christ, are unbelieving when informed of his resurrection.

'When they hear that Jesus was alive and that she [Mary Magdalene] had seen him, they did not believe it' *(Mark 16:11).*

The Resurrection

At Emmaus, they realise this indeed is Christ by his breaking of the bread and giving it to them, his looking up to heaven and his giving of thanks; as these actions parallel those at The Last Supper. Once convinced, the disciples themselves, who had fearfully abandoned him before his death, now openly spread the news about his raising from the dead. If they didn't know this to be true for sure, they wouldn't risk their lives to tell others of this. After all they also recently witnessed the sheer terror of the way in which Christ was cruelly tortured and executed, so would hardly wish for the same fate to befall them.

During this time hundreds of people witness the risen Christ and forty days after he rises from the tomb, Jesus goes with his disciples to Mount Olivet near Jerusalem, telling them that the Holy Spirit will soon be upon them:

'After he said this, he was taken up before their very eyes, and a cloud hid him from their sight. They were looking intently up into the sky as he was going, when suddenly two men dressed in white stood beside them. "Men of Galilee," they said, "why do you stand here looking into the sky? This same Jesus, who has been taken from you into heaven, will come back in the same way you have seen him go into heaven"' *(Acts 1: 9-11).*

Returning to heaven from where he came, Jesus' mission and earthly ministry is now at an end, and two thousand years later his sacrifice and legacy live on. The Christian

The Ascension

faith is as strong as ever in believers who, despite having never met him, have Jesus wholeheartedly in their lives. For this opportunity we must be grateful for the pain-staking record keeping of the authors of the Gospels and their ground-breaking testimonies. But ultimately to Christ our Saviour who suffered unimaginably at the hands of humanity for the sake of offering us redemption and his gift of eternal life.

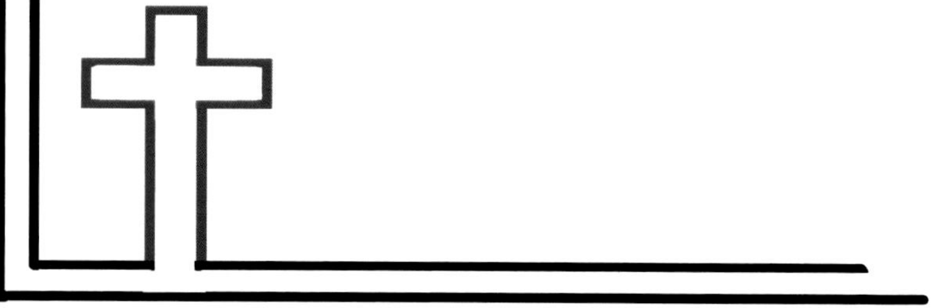

Epilogue

Considering the Resurrection

Jesus being the 'Eternal Son of God' not only came into existence when given a human body, i.e. at the time of his physical birth, but has always existed. Jesus who is given many titles in the Gospels and is referred to as 'The Son of David' *(Luke 1:32)* and 'King of Kings' *(Revelation 17: 14)* as well as many others, is put to death for blasphemy. The very reason for God raising him from the dead was to show that he was innocent of this crime; he was the divine son of God and he is God. Without the resurrection event, Christianity would not exist, because Jesus would have been a mere mortal; proving the very foundations of Christianity to be a lie.

The many people who had turned away from Jesus before the crucifixion, after his resurrection realised they had done wrong in doubting him. Consequently they became loyal followers and spread the good news of his word: He died to save the whole of humanity from their sins, with the message that the kingdom of heaven would be open to them if they believe in and follow Christ.

Records show that more than five hundred

people saw Christ after his resurrection *(1 Corinthians 15:6)*, so it seems unlikely that his rising could be part of an elaborate deception. Many of the believers lost their lives in the process of spreading his word and it seems implausible for them to do this if they did not believe what they were saying. People accepted the witness testimonies and Christianity as a result spread throughout the world. There are many examples in the Gospels of Jesus' companions reporting their own failings, such as on the night of Jesus' death when, although asked by Jesus to stay awake, they failed, and fell asleep *(Luke 22:39-46).* A willingness to admit failings is a good sign of honesty *(Nelson, 2008).*

In the Gospel of Matthew *(28:11-15)*, it is written that once they discovered the tomb empty, the authorities bribed the guards to say that Jesus' disciples had stolen his body while they were sleeping. Now fearful for their lives, they too realised that Jesus was the expected Messiah and they were the ones who had put him to death. The enemies of Jesus would have given anything to produce his corpse, and to prevent the spread of his following, but of course they couldn't. People close enough to know the truth and bear witness to these events and who risked their lives for their faith could not face the prospect of death for hollow propaganda. They knew something magnificent and powerful had happened and with the assistance of the authors of the Gospels, two of whom were apostles of Jesus himself (Matthew and John) the word of Jesus was delivered to others.

Many sceptics argue that if God is so powerful, he wouldn't send his son in the form of Jesus to be crucified then resurrected, thus casting more doubt and questioning of his existence. He would show himself to us all so we know he exists. But this would not be the true faith which God requires us to have. We should believe in him though we have not seen him. As Jesus said to Thomas, at Emmaus,

"Because you have seen me, have you believed? Blessed are they who did not see and yet believed" *(John 20:29).*

Faith is not something which is easy to have, understand or live our lives by. It isn't meant to be. The very fact that we have not seen Jesus, but yet believe, demonstrates true faith eliminating the need for proof. If we have an authentic belief in him we then have the genuine love needed to accept God into our lives, and the ability to live our lives the way he wants us to. Without genuine faith we could not possess this insight nor require or understand it. Faith gives us the motivation to discover and learn about his teachings and places responsibility on ourselves rather than onto God. Furthermore, the resurrection and ascension are necessary elements of the ministry of Jesus Christ, which enable people to see that all those who believe in him will also have eternal life in the kingdom of heaven. Faith is trusting in what we have good reason to believe is true, and all the evidence suggests that the events surrounding Jesus' life, death and resurrection are true; and this authenticates the subsequent rise in Christianity. The early Church was created on the basis of Jesus Christ's existence and by those who were there to bear witness to his resurrection.

The faith and fascination Jesus captured has continued centuries later, and despite the criticism and scepticism, remains strong to this day. But cynicism of course, is not a recent phenomenon, as even when Jesus was on earth people had the same doubts, with even the disciples themselves expressing moments of disbelief. Where cynicism exists regarding the event of the resurrection, this must also be applied to the ascension and all the miracles Jesus performed. These are all supernatural in nature, so if we believe that Jesus healed the sick for example, it is logical that we also believe in the *Ascension, Transfiguration* and *Resurrection,* as explained in the New Testament. They are all events based on the same fundamental principle which cannot be explained by nature as we know it. Jesus' life displays the multitude of sin within the capability of humanity, against the stark contrast of Jesus' divine inner beauty and grace. He forever remains both God and man in divine glory.

(Please see further reading list for in depth investigation into the resurrection and the last days of Jesus).

Something to think about...

Jesus told his followers that he would one day come back to the world and reclaim it for himself and for them. He linked this with the prophecy of Isaiah suggesting that there will be one day be, "a new heaven and a new earth", with the curse described in Genesis removed *(Isaiah 65:17-25, Matthew 19:28)*. He said that there will be increased tribulation first. Then he would come in the manner the prophets had foreseen *(Isaiah 13:10, 34:4, Daniel 7:13-14) (Nelson, 2008, p47)*.

"Approximately 2,500 prophecies appear in the pages of the Bible, about 2,000 of which already have been fulfilled to the letter - no errors. (The remaining 500 or so reach into the future and may be seen unfolding as days go by). Since the probability for any one of these prophecies having been fulfilled by chance, averages less than one in ten (figured very conservatively) and since the prophecies are for the most part independent of one another, the odds for all these prophecies having been fulfilled by chance without error is less than one in 10 2000 (that is 1 with 2000 zeros written after it)" *(Ross, 2003)*.

In fact, the Bible is the only documentation ever discovered which is proven to have written history before it occurred. So we certainly have very good reason to think Isaiah is correct in his prediction. When this will happen is up to God to decide.

Other Book Titles by This Author (Available or Coming Soon):

- **INSPIRATIONAL WOMEN FROM THE BIBLE**
- **IMPROVE YOUR CHURCH:** Attracting a 21st Century Audience
- **THE STORY OF JESUS** (Children's Edition)
- **SCIENCE VS. RELIGION: ARE THEY MUTUALLY EXCLUSIVE?** (Christianity in a Scientific Atheist World)
- **FOOD FOR CHRISTIAN THOUGHT:** Connecting With Christ In Everyday Life
- **CHRISTIAN OR CULT?** Investigating Major Cult Doctrines And Their Contradictions To True Christianity

RESOURCES & FURTHER READING:

Bauckham, R., 2006, *Jesus and the Eyewitness,* Cambridge, U.K, Wm. B. Eerdman's Publishing Co.

Bible Gateway, 2014, *online Bible resource*. Available at: https://www.biblegateway.com/ [Accessed 26 October 2014]

BibleHub, 2014, *online Bible resource.* Available at: http://biblehub.com/timeline/new.htm [Accessed 3 October 2014]

Cru.org, 2014, *online resource.* Available at: http://www.cru.org/ [Accessed 28 November 2014]

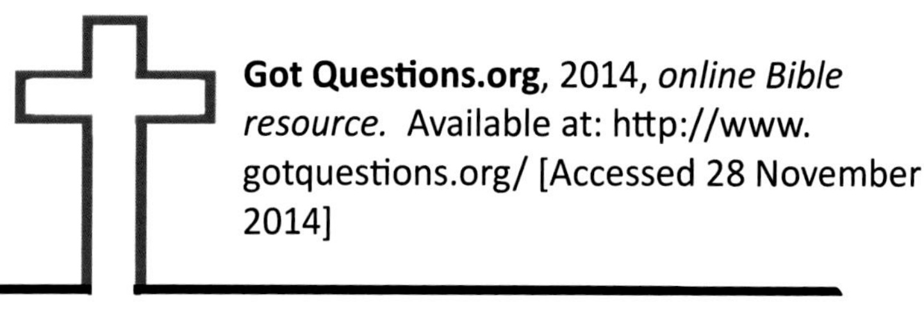

Got Questions.org, 2014, *online Bible resource.* Available at: http://www.gotquestions.org/ [Accessed 28 November 2014]

Habermas, G., Licona, M., 2004, *The Case for the Resurrection of Jesus*, MI, U.S.A, Kregel Publications.

Holy Bible, *New International Version*, 2011. U.K., Hodder & Stoughton Publishers.

Horsfield, E.J., 2015, *Science vs. Religion: Are they Mutually Exclusive? Christianity in an Atheist Scientific World,* U.K., Peace Press.

Loverance, R., 2007, *Christian Art* (The British Museum), London, The British Museum Press.

Nelson, P., 2008, *The Logic of Life: Seeking Truth to Live by.* U.K., Avenue Books.

Nichols, B., 1999, *Free Christian Clip Art.* Online. Available at: http://www.bnichols.pwp.blueyonder.co.uk/freecc/images/index.htm [Accessed 16 February 2015]

O'Reilly, B., 2014, *The Last Days of Jesus*, New York, Henry Holt and Company Publishers.

Ross, H., 2003, *Fulfilled Prophecy: Evidence for the Reliability of the Bible.* Online. Available at: http://www.reasons.org/articles/articles/fulfilled-prophecy-evidence-for-the-reliability-of-the-bible [Accessed 15 January 2015]

Schaeffer, F., 2006, *Art and the Bible.* U.S.A, Intervarsity Press.

Sheen, F.J., 2012, *Life of Christ*, New York, Double Day, Random House Publishing Inc.

Shuckburgh Reynolds Limited, 1993, *The Illustrated Gospels*, U.K., Random House Publishing.

Timeline of Jesus, 2014, *Dates and Events.* Online. Available at: http://www.datesandevents.org/people-timelines/36-timeline-of-jesus.htm [Accessed 19 October 2014]

Vectoropenstock.com, 2014. Online. Available at: https://www.vectoropenstock.com/ [Accessed 22 December 2014]

VectorPortal.com, 2013. Online. Available at: http://www.vectorportal.com/ [Accessed 21 December 2014]

Watts, M., 2014, *The Lion Bible for Children,* Oxford, U.K, Lion Hudson Plc. (HIGHLY RECOMMENDED FOR ABSOLUTE BEGINNERS)

What Christians Want to Know, 2014, *online Bible resource*. Available at: http://www.whatchristianswanttoknow.com/ [Accessed 18 October 2014]

Wilkins, M., Moreland, J., 1994, *Jesus Under Fire,* Michigan, U.S.A, Zondervan Publishing House.